T0057986

Life × 3

Yasmina Reza is a playwright and novelist whose plays have all been multi-award-winning, critical and popular international successes. *Conversations après un enterrement* (*Conversations after a Burial*), Théâtre Paris Villette, Théâtre Montparnasse (1987), Almeida Theatre, London (2000). *La Traversée de l'hiver*, Théâtre du Rond Point, Paris (1990). *'Art'*, Comédie des Champs Elysées (1994), Wyndham's Theatre, London (1996), Royale Theatre, New York (1999). *L'Homme du hasard* (*The Unexpected Man*), Théâtre Hébertot, Paris (1996), Royal Shakespeare Company and Duchess Theatre, London (1998), Promenade Theatre, New York (2000). *Trois versions de la vie* (*Life x 3*), Burgtheater, Vienna (2000), Théâtre Antoine, Paris (2000), Royal National Theatre, London (2000). She translated *La Metamorphose* (Steven Berkoff's version of Kafka's *Metamorphosis*, directed by Roman Polanski). Other writings: *Hammerklavier* (1997 – Prix de la Nouvelle from the French Academy) and *Une Desolation* (1999). Film includes: *Le Pique-nique de Lulu Kreutz* (2000), directed by Didier Martiny.

Christopher Hampton was born in the Azores in 1946. He wrote his first play, *When Did You Last See My Mother?*, at the age of eighteen. His work for the theatre, television and cinema includes *The Philanthropist*, *Tales from Hollywood*, adaptations from Ibsen and Molière and the screenplays *Dangerous Liaisons*, *Carrington* and *The Secret Agent*, the last two of which he also directed.

YASMINA REZA

Life × 3

translated by
Christopher Hampton

FARRAR, STRAUS AND GIROUX

NEW YORK

First published in 2000

Farrar, Strauss & Giroux
18 West 18th Street, New York 10011

Typeset by Country Setting, Kingsdown, Kent CT14 8ES

© Yasmina Reza, 2000
Translation © Yasmina Reza and Christopher Hampton, 2000

Yasmina Reza and Christopher Hampton are hereby
identified as translators of this work in accordance with
Section 77 of the Copyright, Designs and Patents Act 1988

A CIP record for this book
is available from the British Library

ISBN: 978-0-571-20738-1

www.fsgbooks.com

P1

Life × 3 was first presented at at the Lyttelton Theatre,
Royal National Theatre, London, on 7 December 2000.
The cast, in order of speaking, was as follows:

Henri Mark Rylance
Sonia Harriet Walter
Inès Imelda Staunton
Hubert Oliver Cotton

Musician Walter Fabeck (keyboards)

Director Matthew Warchus
Designer Mark Thompson
Lighting Designer Hugh Vanstone
Music Gary Yershon
Sound Designer Christopher Shutt
Company Voice Work Patsy Rodenburg

Yasmina Reza and Christopher Hampton would like
to thank Catherine McMillan for her contribution to
the translation

Characters

Henri
Sonia
Inès
Hubert

Voice of
The Child

LIFE x 3

One

Evening.
  A living room. As abstract as possible. No walls, no doors; as if open to the sky. What's important is the suggestion of a living room.
  Sonia is sitting down, wearing a dressing gown. She's looking through a file. Henri appears.

Henri He wants a biscuit.

Sonia He's just cleaned his teeth.

Henri He's asking for a biscuit.

Sonia He knows very well there's no biscuits in bed.

Henri You tell him.

Sonia Why didn't you?

Henri Because I didn't know there were no biscuits in bed.

Sonia How could you not know there were no biscuits in bed? Biscuits have never been allowed in bed, nothing sweet is.

  She goes out.
  Pause.
  The child starts crying. She comes back.

Henri What's the matter with him?

Sonia He wants a biscuit.

Henri Why is he crying?

Sonia Because I said no. He's getting horribly temperamental.

Slight pause.

Henri Give him a slice of apple.

Sonia He doesn't want a slice of apple, he wants a biscuit, and in any case he's not getting anything. You don't eat in bed, you eat at the table, you don't eat in bed after you've cleaned your teeth and now I need to look through this file, I have a ten o'clock meeting in the morning.

The child continues crying.
  Henri goes out. The child stops crying.
  Henri comes back.

Henri He's agreed to a slice of apple.

Sonia He's not having any apple, he's not having anything, you don't eat in bed, the subject is closed.

Henri You tell him.

Sonia Stop it.

Henri I said yes to the apple, I thought the apple was a possibility. If you're saying no, go and tell him yourself.

Pause.

Sonia Take him in a slice of apple and tell him you're doing it behind my back. Tell him I said no and that you're only doing it because you said yes, but that I mustn't find out because I'm radically opposed to any kind of food in bed.

Henri Should I peel it?

Sonia Yes.

Henri goes out.
  Pause. He comes back.

Henri He wants you to give him a cuddle.

Sonia I've already given him a cuddle.

4

Henri Go and give him a little cuddle.

Sonia How many more times are we supposed to go back in his room?

Henri Just a little cuddle. I calmed him down, he'll go to sleep.

Sonia goes out. Pause.
The child starts crying. She comes back.
She sits down in silence. She picks up her file.

Now what's the matter with him?

Sonia He wants the whole apple.

Pause.
They go back to what they were doing.

Henri Why don't we give him the whole apple? It's good that he likes fruit.

Sonia He's not having any more.

Henri If you like, I'll peel it and take it in to him.

Sonia Spoil him. What do I care? Do what you like.

Henri (*towards the child*) Arnaud, night night!

Sonia He's a pain in the arse.

Henri Night night!

Sonia The more you keep yelling night night the more worked up he gets.

Henri We're not spending the rest of the evening listening to him snivel. I don't understand why you're being so inflexible. What difference is a little apple going to make to the course of history?

Sonia If we give in on the apple, he'll know he can get us to give in on anything.

Henri All you have to do is tell him we're giving in on the apple this evening and this evening only, to be nice to him and because we're tired of listening to him whining.

Sonia Definitely not because we're tired of listening to him whining!

Henri Yes, right, that's what I meant, from now on we're never going to give in again, especially if he whines at the least little rebuff, because that's only going to stiffen our resolve.

Sonia To say we're tired of listening to him whining is the worst possible way of expressing it. It's inconceivable that you could even come up with an expression like that.

Henri We're *tired*, in the general sense of the word, of listening to him whining. Generally speaking, we're up to *here* with the sound of whining.

Sonia Hence the whole apple.

Henri Hence the apple, hence the final, exceptional apple.

> *Sonia reads.*
> *Henri goes out.*
> *Very soon, the child stops snivelling. Henri comes back.*

He was pleased. In fact, you know, I think he really was hungry. I explained to him it was imperative he improve his behaviour. Imperative. He wants a cuddle. Just a little cuddle.

Sonia No.

Henri A little cuddle.

Sonia (*parodying him*) . . . a little cuddle.

Henri I told him you were coming.

Sonia gets up.

(*towards the child*) Mummy's coming!

Sonia goes out.
Henri's on his own.
Quite soon, the child starts crying.
Sonia comes back.

Sonia I'm not going in there one more time, I hope that's clear.

Henri What's happening? Every time you go in there, he cries.

Sonia What's that supposed to mean?

Henri I don't know. Every time you go into his room, he starts crying again.

Sonia So?

Henri When I go in, he calms down and gets ready to go to sleep like a good boy.

Sonia And when I go in, he screams his head off.

Henri What did you say to him?

Sonia To make him scream his head off?

Henri Listen, you must admit it's strange, it's as if you upset him every time you go in.

Sonia You know what he wanted? He didn't want 'a little cuddle', he wanted a story. He wanted to hear a fourth story while he was scoffing his apple.

Henri Arnaud, night night!

Sonia Shut up, Arnaud!

Henri Don't speak to him like that.

Sonia Shut the fuck up, Arnaud!

Henri Are you out of your mind?

Sonia He's stopped. There you are.

Henri He's stopped because he's traumatised.

Sonia You couldn't traumatise anyone, that's for sure. Not your son and not Hubert Finidori.

Henri What's Hubert Finidori got to do with it?

Sonia I'd like to record your voice when you're on the phone with him. Your kow-towing, your obsequious tone of voice.

The Child (*from its room*) Daddy!

Henri Yes, darling! (*on his way out*) Perhaps you'll explain to me what Hubert Finidori is doing in this conversation.

*Sonia's started reading again.
Henri comes back.*

He's very upset.

No reaction from her.

He can't understand how a mother could be so violent.

Sonia Poor little poppet.

Henri Sonia, if you carry on like this and that boy goes on being a pain in the arse, I'm going.

Sonia Go.

Henri I'm going and I'm not coming back.

Sonia Who's stopping you?

Henri wrenches the file out of Sonia's hands and throws it on the floor.

Henri Go and give him a kiss, go and tell him you're sorry you lost all sense of proportion.

Sonia Let go of me!

Henri I won't let you go until you've apologised.

Sonia Apologised for what? You couldn't take my side just for once in your life! Apologised for what? For not having taken him in a packet of chocolate fingers? Do you want a packet of chocolate fingers, Arnaud?!

Henri You're hysterical!

Sonia There's a box of chocolate fingers, Arnaud, you want it?

Henri Stop it!

Sonia Daddy's bringing you a box of chocolate fingers!

Henri is trying to put his hand over her mouth.

The Child (*from its room*) Daddy!

Henri That's enough, Arnaud!

They grapple.

Sonia Why are you telling him that's enough, poor little thing, the chocolate fingers was our idea!

Henri Be quiet!

Sonia You're suffocating me!

Henri He can hear everything!

Sonia Help!

We leave them with brutal abruptness, in mid-action.

*

Evening. The street.

Inès I've laddered my stocking!

Hubert It doesn't show.

Inès Because it's just started. It can only get worse.

Hubert It really doesn't matter.

Inès Hubert, I am not going to visit people I've never met before with a ladder in my stocking.

Hubert We're already half an hour late, we can't go back home, and we can't go shopping for stockings in the middle of the night. Let's just rise above it.

Inès You rushed me and this is what happens. Is it far? Why did you park so far away? There's dozens of spaces, look, who'd want to live out here?

Hubert Haven't you got any nail-varnish?

Inès Nail-varnish?

Hubert To stop the ladder?

Inès And look like some tramp?

Hubert It's twenty past nine.

Inès I cannot turn up with a ladder in my stocking!

Hubert Who's going to notice?

Inès Who's going to notice? Everyone, except for you, if someone turns up at my house with a ladder in her stocking, the ladder's the first thing I notice.

Hubert All you have to do is tell Henri's wife you've just laddered your stocking in the lift, that you're very embarrassed, with any luck she'll lend you one, Inès, we don't give a damn about these people, he hasn't published in three years, he needs my support to be made Research Director, doesn't matter how laddered your stocking is, they'll be licking our boots.

*

Back at Sonia and Henri's.
  They come out of the child's room together.

Henri You've terrified him.

Sonia Henri, we've just discussed all this, don't let's start again.

Henri A six-year-old child, hearing his mother screaming for help. Think about it.

Sonia We calmed him down, the subject is closed.

Henri In his own home! In his own home! Which means the aggressor can only be me. His father.

Sonia Arnaud accepted that we were joking.

Henri To humour us. He's much sharper than you think.

Sonia The subject is closed.

  She plunges back into her files.

Henri So, I'm obsequious when I talk to Hubert Finidori?

  The doorbell rings.

Sonia (*under her breath*) Who's that?

Henri (*under his breath*) I'll go and look.

  He comes back immediately.
  All the following exchanges under their breath.

The Finidoris!

Sonia It's tomorrow!

Henri It's the seventeenth . . . it's this evening.

Sonia This is a catastrophe!

Henri Yes.

Sonia Have they heard us?

Henri Why, what did we say?

Sonia We can't let them in.

Henri We can't not let them in.

Sonia What are we going to do?

Henri Go and . . . go and fix yourself up a bit.

Sonia Are we going to let them in?

Henri They know we're here.

Sonia This is a catastrophe.

Henri Is there anything left in the kitchen?

Sonia We cleaned it out. I thought it was tomorrow.

Henri This was a very important dinner for me!

Sonia You're saying it's my fault!

Henri At least go and change.

Sonia No.

Henri You cannot receive the Finidoris in your dressing gown!

Sonia Yes, I can.

> *Henri pushes her towards the back of the flat, trying not to make any noise.*

Henri Will you go and get dressed, Sonia!

Sonia (*resisting his pressure*) No.

> *They struggle in silence.*

Henri How can you be so selfish?

The bell rings again.

I'm letting them in.

*

Inès, Hubert, Sonia and Henri in the living room.
The two guests are picking at various snacks (crisps,
processed cheese, a box of chocolate fingers, etc.) set out
on a tray. They have drinks, as do Sonia and Henri.
Sonia has changed. Inès still has a ladder in her
stocking.

Inès Me too, I'm very much on top of the mysteries of
bedtime. First of all, the time, we go to bed at eight
o'clock, well, that's to say we can stretch it to half past
eight, but anyway, let's say between eight and half past,
whatever happens, by eight-thirty we are in bed, with
ultra-clean teeth, because, to be honest, in the morning,
I find it difficult to insist they clean their teeth before
school, I realise it's wrong, in fact teeth ought to be
cleaned, at the very least, in the morning and at night,
but there we are, I turn a blind eye in the morning,
whereas at night, they know this is something fundamental
and that obviously eating anything at all afterwards is
out of the question, as for Hubert, it's strange, he's in
agreement with the educational guidelines, but on the
other hand he'll go and get them worked up by starting
a game of football with them, in their room, at eight
o'clock in the evening.

Everyone laughs.

Hubert Once. Once, I played football.

Inès Once you played football, but you regularly get
them worked up.

13

Henri So you're very strict on teeth.

Inès Oh, yes. Yes, very strict on teeth. Basically, it's not so much teeth as discipline. Although I'm obviously very much on top of the hygienic aspect of course, but teeth is discipline. You go to bed, you clean your teeth.

Sonia (*to Henri*) You see!

Henri Arnaud cleans his teeth.

Sonia And then afterwards you peel him an apple.

Inès (*laughing pleasantly*) Oh, no. No! If you peel him an apple after his teeth, the whole system collapses.

Henri When I wash my hands, it's very rare for me not to touch anything afterwards.

Hubert Well done, Henri. Their theories'll be the death of us. What we need is women you can switch off every so often. They're not bad, these little biscuits. (*He munches a chocolate finger.*) So, where have you got to with the flatness of halos?

Henri I've finished. I'm submitting the paper before the end of the month.

Hubert Brilliant. Having said that, you ought to check in Astro PH, I have the impression a similar piece has been accepted by the A.P.J.

The Child (*from its room*) Mummy!

Henri (*shattered*) Oh, yes? Is this very recent?

Hubert Yes, yes, this morning: 'On the Flatness of Galaxy Halos.'

The Child Mummy!

Henri On the flatness of galaxy halos? That's my subject! What's he want, Sonia, go and have a look, darling!

Sonia goes out.

You've got me worried, Hubert.

Hubert Check before you get in a state about it.

Henri I left my laptop at the Institute.

The child starts crying.

Henri What's wrong with him this evening! 'On the Flatness of Galaxy Halos' is my subject! 'Are the Dark Matter Halos of Galaxies Flat?' What's the difference?

Hubert Perhaps he's dealing with visible matter. I just ran my eye over the abstract. (*He munches the last chocolate finger.*) Although I must say it troubled me, that's why I'm telling you about it.

The child's crying is still audible.

Inès Perhaps he should read it before he starts getting upset.

Hubert Inès, my love, don't interrupt when you don't know what you're talking about.

Henri (*loudly*) What's the matter with him, Sonia!

Inès Why depress him in advance?

Sonia comes back.
The child has stopped crying.

Sonia He wants chocolate fingers.

Henri This is insane.

Sonia He's had his apple, now he wants chocolate fingers.

Hubert (*flourishing the empty packet*) I hope he doesn't mean these delicious things I've just been eating.

Sonia He does.

Henri And a good thing too! We're not giving him chocolate fingers in bed at ten o'clock at night.

Hubert I'm appalled. Was that the last packet?

Inès No, listen, Hubert, they're not going to give him chocolate fingers in bed at ten o'clock at night!

Henri Of course we're not.

Sonia We could give him some cheese.

Henri Sonia, what's got into you?

Sonia You'd rather he ruined the evening? At least we'll have a bit of peace.

Inès That's what he's banking on.

Sonia Sorry?

Inès He's making himself obnoxious so that you'll give in.

Sonia And we are giving in.

Inès And you're wrong.

Hubert Look, Inès, don't interfere . . .

Inès I'll interfere any way I like, will you stop trying to muzzle me!

Henri (*to Sonia*) Take him some cheese, take him whatever you like as long as he stops interrupting us! What was his approach? Modelisation of observations or numerical simulation?

Hubert I think it was modelisation, but as I said . . .

Henri (*interrupting him*) Modelisation! I'm fucked. Two years' work blown to fuck.

Hubert Don't go off the deep end, Henri! I say modelisation but maybe it's simulation and in any case maybe he's only modelised the visible areas!

Inès What's your subject in layman's terms?

Henri Are the dark matter halos of galaxies flat?

Inès And are they flat, do you think?

Henri I think they're ten times as thin as they're long.

Inès Right . . .

Sonia comes back.

Sonia He doesn't want cheese, he doesn't want anything, he wants chocolate fingers and you've absolutely not to feel bad about having finished the packet, because we wouldn't have given him any.

Henri What's he doing?

Sonia Crying. I closed all the doors so we wouldn't hear him.

Inès Poor little poppet.

Sonia Have you had enough to eat? I'm so embarrassed.

Henri If it hadn't been for Arnaud, we could have taken you out to dinner.

Hubert Henri, stop looking so lugubrious. Even if your approaches are similar, which is by no means established, you'll undoubtedly have reached different conclusions.

Inès Of course you will!

Hubert See, and she knows what she's talking about!

Inès No one's laughing. Least of all poor Henri.

Hubert I know how to make Henri laugh! Henri, you feel like a laugh, ask Inès to describe a halo for you.

Sonia Henri has his own in-house ignoramus.

Inès I'm not offended, you know!

Henri That paper is my scientific death warrant. It's worrying me, not being able to hear the boy. Open the doors, Sonia, please, I have enough to worry about for one evening!

Inès What do you think's going to happen?

Henri Nothing. But when my son is crying, I prefer to hear it.

Sonia You maybe, but not necessarily our guests.

Inès Open the doors, don't worry about us.

Hubert Don't worry about us.

Sonia goes back towards the child's room.

Anyway, old chap, you seem slightly sensitive this evening. Scientific death warrant!

Sonia comes back. The child is not to be heard.

Henri Three years without publishing, only to see your subject refused because it's already been covered, what do you call that? A scientific death warrant.

Hubert We're not in America!

Henri It's worse here. At least over there you know where you stand. I can't hear him, has he calmed down?

Sonia So it seems.

Henri You didn't go in to see him?

Sonia No.

Henri It's not normal for him to stop crying suddenly just like that.

Inès You mollycoddle him, Henri.

Hubert She's terrible! (*to Inès*) You are, terrible!

Henri Now I'm going to have to start again, to take his work into account. I'm going to have to quote him, I'm going to have to quote him and who's probably going to be asked to report on my paper? Him.

Hubert So what? In six months you'll be telling me he's prepared the best report you've ever had. You must be at the end of your tether, old son, otherwise why make such a song and dance?

Inès (*to Hubert*) What possible reason could you have for telling him about this paper?

Henri Thank God! Thank God he did tell me about it! Thank you, Hubert. Sincerely, thank you.

Sonia What for? For ruining your weekend?

Henri Thank you for tipping me off. Thank you for stopping me looking like a buffoon on Monday morning at the office. I'm sure by now Raoul Arestegui, who lives in front of his screen, has already made a dozen phone calls.

Hubert Frankly, I thought I had to tell you, but I didn't expect this leap into the irrational.

Sonia You could have put it another way.

Hubert Could I? (*He gropes around inside a packet of pistachios, but it's empty.*)

Henri (*with alacrity*) Are there none left? Sonia, you could bring out those little savoury biscuits, would you like something savoury, something savoury or something sweet? What do we have left, darling?

Hubert No, no, you mustn't bother . . .

Sonia You could have warned him some other way, used words which would just leave some vague, inconspicuous scent in the air.

Hubert My dear Sonia, we're in the realm of science. Words are not aromatherapy. Unfortunately.

He's amused himself with this sally and turns to Henri for approval. Henri laughs feebly.

Sonia Whatever realm you claim to inhabit, the words you chose have plunged my husband into disarray.

Hubert It's the facts which have plunged him into disarray. And the disarray is entirely out of all proportion.

Sonia The facts as you presented them. To trigger his disarray.

Henri You're insane. Come on, Sonia, this is ridiculous.

Hubert (*attempting to preserve a good-natured tone*) I shouldn't like to come up against her in court!

Sonia I haven't been in court for years, I work for a finance company.

Hubert But you still know how to use words which . . . how did it go . . .?

Henri Sonia, our friends are still hungry.

Sonia Would you like some Wotsits?

Inès No thanks.

Hubert Ah, yes, Wotsits, I like Wotsits.

Sonia goes out.

Henri Something stronger?

Hubert No, thanks, I'll stick with the Sancerre.

Inès Is it important for halos to be flat?

Hubert Feminine logic! She ticks me off for mentioning it and now she brings up the subject again.

Sonia has returned.

Cheesy Wotsits! My favourite!

Inès Is it important?

Henri When you look at the Milky Way, does it seem to form a straight line? . . .

Inès Yes.

The Child Mummy!

Sonia Night night, Arnaud!

Henri . . . Well, I have serious reasons to suppose that the deployment of invisible matter which surrounds it is more or less as flat as the visible matter.

The Child Mummy! I'm thirsty!

Henri He's thirsty.

Inès What difference does that make?

Henri All the difference in the world. Until today the halo was assumed to be round. It was spherical! (*to Sonia*) You wouldn't like to take him in a little glass of water?

Sonia No.

Inès And what difference does it make if the halo's not round any more?

Henri To our everyday life, none.

Hubert Inès, stop pestering him with your inept questions.

The Child Mummy!

Henri It's a modification of a presumed reality. A new entry in the encyclopaedia of mankind. Sonia, dear, take him in a drink, we can't let him monopolise the evening!

Inès How old is he?

Sonia Six.

Inès Can't he fetch his own drink?

Sonia No.

Henri Yes, he can, of course he can, it's just that we don't like him to get out of bed.

Sonia He does not know how to fetch his own drink.

Henri He absolutely knows how to, but he's not allowed to get out of bed.

Sonia Arnaud does not know how to fetch his own drink.

Henri Of course he does!

Inès A six-year-old knows how to fetch his own drink.

Sonia Not our son.

Henri Arnaud knows perfectly well how to fetch his own drink, come on, Sonia!

Hubert If you ask me he knows how to, but he prefers to be served.

Henri Exactly!

Hubert He's a pasha!

   Sonia goes out.

I haven't upset her, have I?

Henri Of course not.

Inès You're wrong to give in to all his whims.

Hubert Meddling again, Inès.

Inès What do you mean, meddling! Who called him a pasha?

Hubert I called him a pasha as a joke. I'm not telling people what to do.

Henri Two years' work blown to fuck . . .

Hubert Henri, for God's sake!

Henri Three years without publishing, even as a minor collaborator. In America people like that get bounced into teaching.

Sonia returns and heads towards the tray; she's looking for something.

Sonia Are there any more Wotsits?

Henri Who for, for Arnaud?

Sonia He's had his glass of water and he promises not to bother us any more if he can have a plate of Wotsits.

Hubert (*searching*) Don't tell me I've finished the Wotsits!

Henri (*finding one*) Here's one! One left.

Hubert Two!

Henri Two Wotsits, that should do, shouldn't it?

Sonia sets off again with the Wotsits.

Inès (*to Henri*) So you thought it was all your idea?

Hubert What idea, darling?

Inès Hubert, please, stop trying to police everything I say!

Hubert I'm not trying to police everything you say, my darling, I just didn't understand your question . . .

Inès You understood it perfectly well, not that it was addressed to you, but you understood it perfectly well, and this permanently ironic tone you use to greet everything I say as if I were a half-wit is intolerable.

The child starts crying.

Hubert Now you've made him cry.

Henri What's going on, Sonia, shit!

Hubert Calm down, let's all calm down, keep a sense of proportion.

Sonia comes back.

Sonia Two Wotsits wasn't enough, he's had a smacked bottom, I don't wish to discuss it.

Henri Have you closed the doors?

Sonia Yes.

Slight pause.

Hubert Have you been here long?

Sonia A year and a half.

Hubert Where were you before?

Sonia Montparnasse.

Hubert This is better. Quieter.

Sonia Yes.

Hubert And you no longer practise as a lawyer?

Sonia No.

Hubert Henri told me you were a lawyer, I imagined you practised as a lawyer.

Sonia I qualified as a lawyer.

Hubert I see.

Henri A brilliant woman married to a failure.

Hubert Let's pretend we didn't hear that.

Sonia And you, Inès, what do you do?

Inès Nothing. That's to say, hundreds of things, I've never been as busy as I have since I stopped working.

Hubert That's why I never ask her for anything. Never ask a favour from someone who does nothing. They won't have the time. (*He amuses himself with this sally.*)

Inès My husband can only amuse himself at my expense. I can't imagine what would become of him in company if it wasn't for me. (*to Henri*) You haven't answered my question.

Henri Which was?

Hubert Is intergalactic plasma multiphased?

> *He laughs heartily at his own roguishness.*
>   *Sonia laughs involuntarily.*
>   *Henri joins in late.*
>   *Inès is stone-faced.*

Henri (*as the laughter of the other two continues*) You were asking me if other people had tackled my subject.

Inès Thank you, Henri.

Henri I thought I was the first to set about trying to solve it. Even if the question was topical.

Inès You told me your discovery was no use to our everyday life.

Hubert Topical means in the air, my love, in the spirit of the age. Oh, look, there's one more Wotsit!

Sonia Eat it.

Hubert You're joking. I'm in enough trouble with the boy as it is. Having said that, when we start to travel among the galaxies in a thousand years' time, we'll have to take account of Henri's calculations.

Henri Or those of my rival.

The Child (*in a desperate howl*) Daadeee! Daadeeee! . . .

Henri For God's sake, I've had enough, I'm going to bash his head in! Excuse me, two minutes . . . (*He starts to leave.*)

Sonia I'm coming with you.

Hubert Give him the Wotsit, give him the Wotsit!

> *Ridiculously, Henri comes back to get the Wotsit.*
> *They go out.*
> *Inès and Hubert are on their own.*
> *They speak under their breath.*

Hubert They're insane.

Inès Especially him.

Hubert And the child is horrendous.

Inès He has no guidelines, they give him cheese at ten o'clock at night.

Hubert And we've been fed crap.

Inès Why do you put me down in front of other people? I wish I could understand this pathological need you have to continually put me down in front of other people.

Hubert I don't put you down, I was joking.

Inès 'Ask Inès to describe a halo for you,' you think that's hilarious?

Hubert I was just trying to lighten the atmosphere, you saw the state he was in.

Inès Whose fault is that?

Hubert Inès, I'm not going to put up with this recital . . .

Inès Sh! . . .

Hubert (*resumes in a muffled and therefore even more exasperated voice*) . . . this recital of grievances every time we go out somewhere . . .

Inès Did you have to tell him about that paper?

Hubert Now you're shouting.

Inès That man's a depressive.

Hubert I'm not surprised.

Inès What do you mean?

Hubert In a competitive system, it's not having good ideas that counts, it's winning the race. He can kiss goodbye to his promotion.

Henri (*offstage*) One more word, one more squeak and I'll carry out my threat!

Inès How can you be so cold?

Hubert I'm not cold, he's doomed. There are people who are doomed, it's sad but there's nothing you can do about it. You know it's really impossible, that ladder in your stocking, it's been driving me mad ever since we arrived.

Inès lashes out at him, a despairing blow.

Inès Who made me come up like this? I knew it looked awful.

Sonia comes back.

Sonia Who's doomed? My husband?

Hubert Henri?! Doomed? Are you joking? He's the only one who thinks he's doomed! We were talking about our friend Serge Bloch, who, after being flooded out . . .

Inès (*interrupting him*) We were talking about Henri.

27

Hubert (*cheerily*) There's a real wind of madness blowing through this place tonight! She hates me because I've just pointed out she has a ladder in her stocking.

Inès (*extremely animated*) You have not just pointed it out, this stocking was laddered in the street and I didn't want to appear in front of your friends looking like a tinker, I was acutely embarrassed arriving in your flat like this, I was getting ready to apologise and ask you to lend me a pair of stockings, but since you were embarrassed yourself to find us turning up tonight instead of tomorrow, I opted to behave as if nothing was wrong, an aristocratic stance which cost me blood, because, and of course there's no reason you should know this, I'm very particular as a rule, and my husband, instead of supporting me in this course of action, instead of protecting my dignity, can find nothing better to do than attack me in the middle of a conversation by saying the ladder in my stocking is impossible and that I've ruined his evening . . .

Hubert I'm afraid Inès may have somewhat overdone it with the Sancerre!

Inès Don't humiliate yourself by pretending I'm a drunk, Hubert, your usual snide remarks will be quite sufficient . . .

Sonia I only have black stockings, I don't have any flesh-coloured, I don't know if they would do . . .

Inès Everything's fine. Don't worry about me, in any case I'm quite happy to go on wearing something which is ruining my husband's evening . . .

Henri (*on his way back*) The slightest squeak, the slightest disturbance, and you can say goodbye to your mini-cassette!

Hubert Well done!

Henri It's been rather a disjointed evening, hasn't it? I am sorry.

Sonia (*to Inès*) You know, not that it matters, but to tell you the truth I was going to receive you in my dressing gown, Henri begged me to get changed, said I couldn't receive the Finidoris in my dressing gown.

Hubert Such a stickler for formalities, Henri!

Sonia Only when it's you, normally my husband couldn't give a bugger for formalities, except when it's you. But when it's Hubert Finidori, my husband adopts a Finidorian tone, bows down and wants people to get changed.

Henri What do you mean, I bow down, what do you mean, a Finidorian tone, what are you talking about? What are you talking about, Sonia?!

Hubert And why do I deserve this special treatment? Please note I'm affecting to be unaware of the bile sloshing about behind all this.

Sonia The special treatment is because my husband imagines you're capable of having him promoted to Grade A.

Hubert Grade A! She knows what she's talking about, then, she's mastered the jargon.

Inès Hubert!

Henri Sonia, I'm appalled!

Hubert Henri is R.A. at the I.A.P. and I'm lab-director at Meudon, in what way could I be responsible for his recruitment?

Sonia You're a member of the National Committee, you can approve the promotion of people who don't work in your lab.

Henri Hubert, I don't know who's jerking her lead, this is all ridiculous, I'm terribly sorry.

Sonia An example of the Finidorian tone.

Henri Sonia!

Sonia It's obvious you're never going to do anything for my husband, you're enjoying watching him squirm, you warned him about the paper by this competitor with the sole aim of seeing him flounder, thus absolving yourself of all responsibility in the event of his taking it upon himself to come crawling to you to ask for a favour. I find your perversity disgusting and I despise your pathetic string-pulling.

Inès My husband has been published in *Nature* magazine, I fail to see what's pathetic about that.

Hubert Inès, Inès, I really don't need your help, darling.

Henri Hubert is one of the greatest cosmological authorities in the world, there isn't a single paper on galaxy clusters which fails to mention him, so what do you know about it, Sonia? What are you talking about?

Sonia He just said you were doomed.

Hubert She's terrible! I can see why you tend to be slightly erratic, old man.

Henri What do you mean, doomed? Me, doomed?

Sonia That's what he just said. That you were doomed and there was nothing anybody could do for you.

Henri Who to? To you?

Sonia To her.

Inès Hubert was talking about Serge Bloch, you were talking about Serge Bloch, weren't you, Hubert? . . .

Henri What does Serge Bloch have to do with this?

Inès Well, first he was flooded out . . .

Hubert (*interrupting her*) Please, Inès, let's not make ourselves completely idiotic! First of all, Sonia, let me tell you that you'd have done better to receive us in your dressing gown. For one thing, it would have put the finishing touch to the incongruities of the occasion, but above all it would have made you more human. There's something dry and brittle about you, which is in total contrast to the pretty and flirtatious woman you first appear to be.

Henri Couldn't agree more!

Sonia I'd have done better to receive them in my dressing gown?

Inès You'd have done better not to receive us at all! This is the worst evening I've ever spent! (*She shows signs of preparing to leave.*)

Henri Congratulations, Sonia! Well done!

Hubert It's not her fault this evening's been a catastrophe, we've all played our part. Inès, angel, calm down.

Inès Don't call me angel and stop being so smarmy.

Henri Hubert, be honest, am I doomed?

Hubert . . . You're going through a rough patch.

Henri In other words, I'm doomed.

Hubert . . . You're not doomed, you're abnormally anxious and you're completely defeatist, Henri, perhaps you ought to get some help.

Henri Did you really say I was doomed?

Hubert Of course not!

Henri And do you think I still have a chance of being published?

Hubert Certainly! Perhaps not in the A.P.J., but in A. & .A. Or in M.N.R.A.S., I don't see why not.

Inès You couldn't care less whether halos are flat or not, you just want to get published.

Hubert Everyone wants to get published, sweetheart, that's the whole point.

Henri If my paper is turned down, I'm finished.

Hubert You are Research Assistant, you have tenure.

Henri An unsackable failure, what could be worse?

Sonia When I married Henri I imagined – talk about stupid – that there was some ultimate nobility in living among the stars and that it would grant me a certain spiritual loftiness.

Hubert My dear, nothing is in itself elevating or transcendent. Man alone can decide on what he is.

Sonia Brilliant!

Inès Why do you resent my husband?

Sonia I don't resent your husband, it's my husband I resent.

Henri May we know why?

Sonia My husband crawls in front of yours. No normal woman can bear that. Especially when he's a crawler for no good reason.

Henri I absolutely am not a crawler! Am I a crawler, Hubert?!

Inès Let's go, Hubert, this is ghastly.

Henri Hubert, am I a crawler?!

Sonia You're a crawler.

Hubert We're all a bit tiddly . . .

Sonia Don't try to smooth things over, he crawls in front of you, and you take a malicious pleasure in it, which I can understand . . .

Inès How can you humiliate your husband like this?!

Hubert Inès, stop meddling!

Inès I'll meddle as much as I like, shit!

With brutal abruptness, a song, at maximum volume, starts blaring out of the child's room.

Henri What's that?

Sonia The Fox and the Hound. You put the Fox and the Hound on for him. (*She goes off towards the room.*)

Inès He has his own TV?

Henri Not a TV, a mini-cassette, he's allowed to listen to one mini-cassette every evening in bed.

Hubert And if his parents wanted him to watch TV, he'd watch TV!

Inès I didn't say he shouldn't watch TV!

Hubert Yes, you did. You didn't say it but you thought it. You have a propensity for making rules even when it's none of your business.

Inès Did I say he shouldn't watch TV?!

Henri He's not watching TV! He's listening to a little mini-cassette in the dark!

Sonia comes back; the music is no longer to be heard.

Sonia He says we're keeping him awake.

Inès He's right, we are keeping him awake, let's go, Hubert.

Henri Before I let you go, Hubert, I want to know if you think I'm a crawler?!

Hubert You're keeping him awake, Henri.

Henri (*lowering his voice*) Am I a crawler?

Hubert (*lowering his voice*) A bit.

Henri A bit!

Inès You asked for it! And it's true, you're a crawler! Hubert, I can't take any more!

Hubert You lack a certain size, Henri, I'm very sorry. You seem somehow adrift, unfocused, maybe you should take a few lessons from your wife, let's go.

They leave.
Henri and Sonia are on their own.

Two

Evening.
  The same room.
  Sonia is sitting down, wearing a dressing gown. She's looking through a file. Henri appears.
  An atmosphere of calm.

Henri He wants a biscuit.

Sonia He's just cleaned his teeth.

Henri So he has.

  Pause.
    She's looking at her file again, he's hovering indecisively.

Henri How about a slice of apple?

Sonia What's the difference between a slice of apple and a biscuit?

Henri . . . Less sugar in the apple.

Sonia There's a lot of sugar in an apple. Maybe more than in a biscuit.

Henri He often gets hungry in bed, have you noticed? Do you think we feed him too early?

Sonia He eats at half past seven, like any child of his age.

Henri Suppose he cleaned his teeth afterwards?

Sonia What do you mean, afterwards?

Henri After the biscuit. He could eat a biscuit and clean his teeth afterwards.

Sonia All he has to do is eat a biscuit just before going to bed, i.e., just before cleaning his teeth.

Henri Yes.

Sonia You shouldn't have given him that biscuit.

Henri I didn't give him anything.

Sonia Yes, you did.

Henri Half a chocolate finger. That's nothing. I was ruthless.

Slight pause.

So what'll I say to him?

Sonia What'll you say to him?

Henri Shall I say no apple?

Sonia You've just given him a chocolate finger. He's not going to get a chocolate finger and an apple.

Henri I'll tell him no apple.

Sonia Tell him no apple, say night night.

Henri Night night.

He goes out and comes back.

He was so sweet. I put on the Fox and the Hound for him. (*Pause.*) What shall we give them for starters?

Sonia Grapefruit?

Henri Bit pathetic, isn't it?

Sonia Prosciutto melone?

Henri With the lamb?

Sonia (*indicating her file*) Listen, Henri . . .

Henri Prosciutto melone.

Pause.

What about artichokes?

Sonia Fine.

Henri Artichokes or prosciutto melone?

Sonia Henri!

Henri Or what about crab salad? Bit more profile.

Sonia Crab salad. Perfect.

Henri Crab and lamb? . . . Why not? Do you think Finidori's attractive?

Sonia I doubt I've seen him twice in my life.

Henri And did you think he was attractive?

Sonia Arrogant.

Henri Attractive, in other words.

Sonia No, arrogant.

Henri When a woman says arrogant, she means attractive. She might even mean very attractive.

Sonia (*laughing*) Rubbish!

The bell rings.

(*under her breath*) Who's that?

Henri I'll go and look.

He comes back immediately.
All the following exchanges under their breath.

Henri The Finidoris!

Sonia It's tomorrow!

Henri It's the seventeenth . . . it's this evening.

Sonia This is a catastrophe.

Henri Yes.

Sonia What are we going to do?

Henri We can't not let them in.

Sonia I'll go and change.

Henri You haven't got time, you're fine like that.

Sonia I'm not going to receive the Finidoris in my dressing gown.

Henri Who gives a fuck? They might as well see you in your dressing gown, all they're going to get to eat is crisps.

Sonia I'm not letting them in in my dressing gown!

Henri clings on to her dressing gown as the bell rings again.

Henri You haven't got time to change, Sonia!

Sonia (*trying to free herself*) Let me go!

Henri How can you be so selfish?

The bell rings again.

*

Inès, Hubert, Sonia and Henri in the living room.
The two guests are picking at various snacks (crisps, processed cheese, a box of chocolate fingers, etc.) set out on a tray. They have drinks, as do Sonia and Henri.
Sonia has changed. Inès has a ladder in her stocking.

Inès . . . She's alcoholic and depressive. Hubert says it's the same thing but you can be an alcoholic without being a depressive, and depressives aren't all alcoholics, but her, she's both, she takes anti-depressants and she drinks, anyway she arrived at the house, Coco the Clown, blotchy foundation, lipstick all over her face, Serge Bloch bringing up the rear, grinning as if everything was all right – except they'd just been flooded out – she'd hardly sat down before she demanded a Scotch, I look at Serge, no reaction!

Brief silence.

Hubert What are you trying to say, darling?

Inès I just want to point out how little you men care about our dignity.

Henri You couldn't live with Serge Bloch and not be a depressive.

Sonia They were flooded out?

Hubert The kid upstairs, before he went on holiday, watered his plants and left the tap on.

Inès Francine had just redecorated.

Sonia Poor thing! Just her luck!

She laughs heartily. The others join in. Except for Inès.

Hubert Changing the subject, Henri, where have you got to with the flatness of halos?

They munch chocolate fingers.

Not bad, these little biscuits.

Henri I've finished. I'm submitting the paper before the end of the month.

Hubert Terrific. Having said that, you ought to check in Astro PH, I have the impression a similar piece has been accepted by the A.P.J.

Henri Recently?

Hubert This morning. 'On the Flatness of Galaxy Halos.'

Henri On the flatness of galaxy halos!

Sonia (*charmingly*) What's this, Hubert, you're not trying to demoralise my husband?

Hubert In my opinion, Sonia, it would take more than this to demoralise Henri.

Inès So what is your subject?

Henri The same. 'Are the Dark Matter Halos of Galaxies Flat?'

Inès And what does that mean?

Henri There are halos of dark matter in the galaxies, we're trying to establish if they're flattened or spherical.

Inès So which are they?

Hubert Inès, sweetheart, what are these questions, you don't know the first thing about it.

Inès I'm interested in Henri's work.

Hubert She's never been interested in mine. You've made a big impression on her, old man!

Henri I'm doomed.

Sonia (*still cheerful*) Henri, please!

Hubert Don't let's exaggerate! I just ran my eye over the abstract, maybe he's tackling elliptical galaxies . . .

Henri Has he modelised?

Hubert Possibly.

Henri Then he must be talking about spiral galaxies!

Hubert Perhaps he's dealing with visible matter, we don't know what his conclusions might be . . .

Henri I'm doomed! I publish nothing for three years and this bastard pips me to the post at the very moment I'm about to submit. That's what I call doomed!

The Child Daddy!

Sonia He wants you to rewind the cassette.

Inès How old is he?

Sonia Six.

Inès (*to Henri, who is getting ready to leave the room*) May I see him?

Henri Come with me.

They go out.
Hubert and Sonia are on their own.

Hubert That gives me exactly fifteen seconds to persuade you to have lunch with me this week.

Sonia That's more than enough.

Hubert Tomorrow?

Sonia I can't, tomorrow.

Hubert Monday?

Sonia All right.

Hubert Are you coming for his sake or mine?

Sonia For his sake, of course.

Hubert Perfect!

Sonia Why tell him about that paper?

Hubert Sudden inspiration. To spice up the evening.

Sonia So you made it up?

Hubert No.

Sonia Is it serious?

Hubert Depends.

He seizes her hand and lifts it boldly to his lips.

Sonia On what?

Hubert His approach.

Sonia I'll tell him everything.

Hubert Goodbye Grade A!

Sonia laughs.

Sonia He asked me if I found you attractive.

Hubert Did you say very?

Sonia I said arrogant.

Hubert Well done, much more subtle.

Sonia In your circle, do you pass for attractive?

Hubert There's very little competition.

Sonia You're not ashamed?

Hubert Ashamed?

Sonia In my home. Six feet away from your wife.

Hubert My morality is not dictated by distance.

Sonia What is it dictated by?

Hubert You'll find out on Monday.

Inès (*on her way back*) He said, I don't want her in my room. I said, hello, Arnaud, he turned to his father and said, I don't want her in my room. Don't worry about it, I have two of my own, not to mention nephews, I'm not in the least upset.

Sonia I hope Henri told him off.

Inès I need a drink. Thank God, Henri did not tell him off, he went to peel him an apple.

Sonia I bust a gut to get him to clean his teeth and the next minute Henri's stuffing him with food.

Inès Men, they all do that.

Hubert What's this grotesque generalisation about men? Where do you get these ideas, Inès? Personally, I've never stuffed anyone with food.

Inès You get them worked up, which is worse. He can start a game of football when they're just about to get into bed.

Hubert Once, I played football with them, she's going to be talking about it for the next ten years.

Sonia You play football? It's funny, I never imagined you playing football.

Hubert I don't play football, I kick a ball about from time to time with my sons, Inès calls that playing football, how did you imagine me?

Sonia I didn't imagine you. Your husband's a bit full of himself, isn't he?

Inès My husband likes to provoke, if there's a pretty woman in the room, he'll give us his lady-killer.

Hubert The Sancerre going down well, is it, darling?

Henri (*coming back*) I found some Wotsits, I'm so embarrassed, there's a tin of sardines as well, would you like me to open the sardines?

Hubert Wotsits, marvellous. Perhaps I should have gone easier on the chocolate fingers.

Sonia You gave him an apple?

Henri I peeled him a small apple. He's hungry, if he's hungry in bed, what else am I supposed to do?

Sonia You'd already given him a chocolate finger.

Henri Half a chocolate finger. Don't let's start this conversation again, Sonia, it can't be very interesting for our guests.

Hubert Don't you believe it, Henri, a brush with a couple's private life, rather stimulating.

Henri Perhaps, if you were to find a less mundane example.

Hubert That's exactly what's exciting about it. Mundane private life. You can't always fix your mind on higher planes.

Inès Personally, I'm much more intellectually involved in a discussion on the advisability of half a chocolate finger than on the flatness of galaxies.

Hubert Halos, darling.

Henri If we could possibly avoid this subject, if we could possibly completely banish this subject for the evening, I'd be extremely grateful.

Hubert You're tormenting yourself for no good reason, Henri.

Henri I'm not tormenting myself in the slightest, you've been kind enough to inform me of the existence of parallel studies, I've taken note of it, the subject is closed.

Sonia Hubert, it's your duty to reassure my husband. You're responsible for his disarray.

Henri Please, Sonia, will you stop making me out to be someone who gets demoralised at the drop of a hat and who has no backbone whatsoever, everything's fine, we've just got rid of two unpromising subjects, and somewhere between apples and dark matter, I'm sure we can find some new, more beguiling topic.

Hubert Last month, I left to spend a few days at an international conference in Finland. I rubbed shoulders with the best teams in the world. I attended some extraordinary seminars, I gave one myself which was fortunately considered significant, I had the most fruitful encounters with various great pundits and what do I remember? What was it that impressed itself on my mind and, at the risk of seeming pompous, my soul? A drab and lugubrious walk on the outskirts of Turku. I rubbed shoulders with the greatest American, English and Dutch researchers, we had these remarkable encounters and what remains? A dreary walk beside a grey sea.

Pause.

Inès May we know why you're suddenly telling us this?

Hubert It's an echo of what Henri was saying. I was thinking about the relative importance of things. About what's interesting and what isn't. Apparently empty moments stay incised in the memory, trivial words can engage your whole being. Henri? . . .

Sonia Henri? . . . Hubert is making an effort to find us a beguiling subject.

Henri Very beguiling, yes. Go on.

Hubert I've finished.

Slight pause.

Inès Have you lived here long?

Sonia A year and a half.

Hubert Where were you before?

Sonia Montparnasse.

Inès This is better. Quieter.

Henri It's certainly not quiet, they're building a car park in rue Langelot.

Inès It'll be finished at some point.

Henri In two years' time.

Sonia (*laughing*) Next month!

Inès Do you mind if I smoke?

Henri I'd rather you didn't.

Sonia What's bugging you, you're joking! Of course you can smoke, Inès!

Hubert No one's smoking, why do you have to smoke?

Sonia She can absolutely smoke, Henri, tell her she can smoke!

Hubert We're in Henri's flat, cigarettes make Henri uncomfortable, there's no reason Inès should smoke. Added to which, smoking is never an essential for a woman.

Inès I won't smoke.

Sonia Inès, I insist that you smoke.

Inès I don't feel like smoking any more.

Sonia Are you planning to be bad-tempered and rude all evening, Henri?

Henri Smoke, fuck it.

Hubert Henri, I don't want to rub salt in the wound, but you must admit that something's gone wrong with this evening.

A muffled song is heard, coming from the child's room.

Inès The Fox and the Hound!

Henri You really fucking depressed me with your walk in Finland.

Inès Our children have that too.

Henri In my position, Hubert, ludicrous as it may seem, an invitation to Turku is an end in itself. And someone who sees the conference as an end in itself has trouble getting his head around some existential stroll along the Baltic. Should he be listening to a tape this late?

Sonia You just rewound it for him.

Inès Doesn't he know how to rewind his own cassettes?

Sonia He's too lazy to move.

Inès Really?!

Hubert 'Luminous and Dark Matter in Spiral Galaxies', that was the subject of the conference. Why didn't you sign up for it?

Henri To stand in front of a wall poster? And spend twenty-four hours on the sidelines, like Serge Bloch in Edinburgh?

Hubert Your work on the dynamics of galaxies is well known, you'd have had no difficulty getting yourself invited, Henri. Dynamicists were welcome in Turku.

Henri Stop being so condescending. If you don't mind. Stop trying to throw me a lifeline every two minutes. I don't give a fuck about Turku.

Hubert You've just said the opposite.

Henri I don't give a fuck about Turku.

Sonia Stop it, Henri, this is puerile. And embarrassing.

Henri I don't give a fuck about Turku.

Sonia Right, he doesn't give a fuck about Turku, and I wouldn't mind another drop of Sancerre.

Hubert You do give a fuck about Turku, and about your paper, and about your promotion, but you think it's clever – God knows why – to self-destruct out of pride.

Henri You're right, I'm self-destructing in front of you and I'm enjoying it. An hour ago I was all set to kiss your feet, now I'm experiencing the elation of the convert.

Sonia You've had too much to drink, Henri. You're blind drunk.

Henri What? I thought you'd be delighted, darling. Farewell the Finidorian tone. Farewell the head hung low and the hunched shoulders, farewell the servile chuckle . . .

Inès What is the Finidorian tone?

Henri A tone of voice I used to adopt when I believed Hubert Finidori was in a position to determine my future, before he arrived at my flat a day early and lost no time – no time whatsoever! – in giving me a piece of disturbing information, in the vaguest and therefore most disturbing way, and, seeing how disturbed I was, backtracked marginally in order to restore me to reason and then, just to finish the job and steamroller me completely, started boasting about the futility, emptiness and pointlessness of success.

Inès If we did come a day early, Henri, it's entirely my fault. I wrote down Thursday the seventeenth on a scrap of paper when the seventeenth is a Friday, usually on Fridays I have my course at . . .

Hubert We don't care, Inès, we don't care, it's not important. You're a real artist, Henri, you make and unmake the world according to your mood. You raised me to the rank of protector, I had no idea. I had no idea you'd inflicted this status on me. Had I known, I should have made an effort to inform you of my powerlessness. You see, I failed to notice the servile chuckle, and, fool that I am, I discerned a hint of friendship in what was actually the Finidorian tone. I'm sorry you feel so bitter and I'm sorry I can't take responsibility for it, because I had no idea who I was in your eyes.

Inès You had a very clear idea, Hubert, and I've had enough of being insulted every time I open my mouth. Just now, in the street, my husband told me Henri needed his support if he wanted to be made Research Director.

Hubert I did not say, my darling, that Henri needed my support, I said, but you were concentrating on the ladder in your stocking (which by the way, is getting worse), I said, in a spirit of solidarity, that I could conceivably, if Henri managed to publish within the year, give a modest nudge to his promotion prospects. I said it without suspecting this task had already been assigned to me and I said it in the way a man does when he's speaking to his wife in the privacy of a close and trusting relationship.

Sonia Your nerve is disarming. Is this all part of your seductiveness?

Henri Your seductiveness, Hubert! What about that?

Inès You said Henri needed your support. And you also said he and his wife would be licking our boots.

Hubert I was wrong! As you can see, they're by no means licking our boots.

Henri I'm not licking your boots, because I delight in disappointing people,.and as for my wife, I doubt she'd ever lick anyone's boots for my benefit. There are no more chocolate fingers, have you scoffed the entire packet?

Sonia Don't have any more to drink, Henri.

Henri I very much like your tie, Hubert, it's something I noticed at once when you arrived, the splendour of your tie and its failure to match your pocket handkerchief, a remarkably bold gesture, not to mention the very fact of the tie itself, rare in our field, where slovenliness is just one informality among many, but you, Hubert, you're a man from another mould, a man with bearing, remote, formal, melancholy on a northern coastline . . . To be such an insignificant part of the universe and yet to feel the urge to sound your note, your infinitesimal note in the bell-tower of eternity . . .

Inès Listen, as far as I'm concerned – and I've had just as much to drink as you have, Henri, so here goes – I don't agree at all, you'll probably laugh, but what's the difference, my husband guffaws or sighs every time I open my mouth – our relationship's going down the toilet, we may as well admit it – I don't agree at all that man is such an insignificant part of the universe. Where would the universe be without us? A dreary, black place without an ounce of poetry. We're the ones who gave it a name, us, man, we're the ones who provided this labyrinth with black holes and dead stars, with infinity and eternity, with things that no one can see, we're the ones who've made it vertiginous. We're not insignificant, our time may be fleeting, but we're not insignificant . . .

Brief silence.

Sonia You said we'd be licking your boots? I'm sorry to bring things down to earth when Inès has made a valiant attempt to raise the level of debate.

Hubert Licking our boots? Is that a turn of phrase from my vocabulary book?

Inès You said licking our boots.

Hubert I said *licking our boots*, Inès? What does licking our boots mean? Servile, or quite simply, courteous, well brought up? For some obscure reason, Inès stabs me in the back, she flings up some out-of-context remark in her driest and most withering manner and I'm supposed to come up with some response? Surely, dear friends, we're not about to lapse into the completely abject?

Sonia Give up this flatulent tone, Hubert, you're the only one who finds it amusing. You said we'd be licking your boots, and in the phrase, let me point out, it's the *we* which is particularly unfortunate. I can understand you might envisage the suppliant licking your boots, that might even be what constitutes the charm of a suppliant, but to include his wife in this tableau of prostration is a mistake. I did find you somewhat intriguing, I must admit, and I wasn't expecting you to be so crass and ordinary . . .

Henri And you can give up this tone as well, Sonia! What's all this simpering? The charm of a suppliant? If you go on like that, the suppliant might very well punch you in the mouth!

Hubert You've jumped the rails, Henri!

Inès He has not jumped the rails.

Sonia What's the matter with you, Inès?

Inès I saw you just now.

Sonia Saw who?

Inès The two of you.

Sonia Saw what?

Inès You know very well.

Hubert Inès, come down to earth, sweetheart. Inès can't drink more than one glass, after that she can no longer navigate the known universe.

Sonia Saw what? Say it.

Inès You're too strong for me, Sonia, I'm easily demolished . . .

She holds out her glass to Henri, who fills it and empties his own glass.

Inès Thank you, Henri.

Hubert I'll take her home.

Inès It's going to be horrendous in the car, you see, Henri, here he holds back, he behaves like a gentleman, but in the car it'll be a nightmare, would you mind calling me a taxi? . . .

Henri Saw what, Sonia? What did she see?

Sonia What did she see? I don't know! She won't tell us!

Hubert She saw nothing, she's had a little too much to drink and she's going to go home and go quietly to bed . . .

Inès (*to Henri*) They're like each other, they have the same cynicism and the same self-assurance. We can't compete with people like that.

Henri Don't put us in the same category! Don't even think of trying to lump us together! You and I come from separate worlds!

Inès That's what you think . . .

Hubert Let's go.

Henri Fuck off. Take your Hausfrau. And fuck off.

Inès Wonderful, Henri! Call me all the names you can think of, I've gone through the drunkenness barrier, I look like a gypsy, my husband's a swine, for me this is a historic evening . . .

Hubert Let's go.

Inès Yes, let's go, sweetheart, you can finish me off in the Audi, we have a new Audi, Hubert parked it just so about a mile away so it wouldn't get scratched . . .

Hubert You're like Francine Bloch, Inès, you're not going to give us your Francine Bloch, are you, darling!

Inès I'm unhumiliatable, say what you like . . .

Henri And no snivelling! For God's sake! Don't go sentimentalising everything with a lot of suburban whingeing. Unhumiliatable! I like the word, mind you, it's my kind of word, great position to be in, unhumiliatable, fuck off.

Hubert Let's go. (*He drags Inès away.*) See you soon, Sonia.

Sonia Goodbye.

Hubert Monday?

Sonia Absolutely not.

> *He smiles at her.*
> *Hubert and Inès leave.*
> *Henri and Sonia are on their own.*

Three

Evening.
   The four of them (the Finidoris have arrived).
   The same situation.
   Sonia is in her dressing gown.
   Inès has no ladder in her stocking. The atmosphere is relaxed.

Hubert Might there be some sort of overall Theory? A theory unifying all the fundamental forces? You see, even if you could conceive a theory which covered all the basic interactions, for one thing your theory would be far from comprehensive, as Poincaré said, you can examine each individual cell of an elephant, but that won't help you grasp its zoological reality, and you still wouldn't have eliminated the paradox of the cosmos! How can we grasp the world *as it is*? How can we close the gap between reality and representation, the gap between object and word, what are these, chocolate fingers, delicious, how, in short, can we think of the world without our thinking being part of the world?

Henri All the more tragic a paradox since the principal aim of scientific enterprise is total objectivity.

Hubert In imitation of religion and philosophy, science is now chasing the idea of unity. Is it a hopeless pursuit or the promised land?

Henri Who can say?

Sonia What's the aim of a unifying theory?

Hubert It's a good question. A very good question, but I don't know if it's right to speak of aims rather than longings. Our life is full of regrets for an integrated world, nostalgia for some lost wholeness, nostalgia which is accentuated by the fragmentation of the world brought about by modern life.

Henri Quite.

A muffled song is heard, coming from the child's room.

Inès The Fox and the Hound!

Henri How come he's still awake?

Sonia He's awake. You can't force him to sleep. He's turned the light out and he's listening to his cassette.

Inès He's sweet. Very independent.

Sonia Yes, he's very independent.

Inès You're lucky, ours are quite capable of showing up fourteen times in the course of the evening.

Henri Arnaud is entirely self-sufficient. Too much so, perhaps. If you ask me, it's time he turned off his cassette, don't you think, Sonitchka?

Sonia (*getting up, to Inès*) Would you like to see him?

Inès Love to!

They go out.
Hubert and Henri are on their own.

Hubert So, the flatness of halos?

Henri Finished. I'm submitting the paper end of the month.

Hubert Great. Having said that, you ought to check in Astro PH, I have the impression a similar piece has been accepted by the A.P.J.

Henri That's right, 'On the Flatness of Dark Halos in Galaxies', Raoul Arestegui, a colleague of mine, phoned to tell me about it, I left my laptop at the Institute.

Hubert Pretty close to your subject, isn't it? These biscuits are a disaster, take them away.

Henri No, please, tuck in, I'm embarrassed to receive you this way, it's precisely my subject, apparently it's *the* fashionable subject, a Mexican team.

Hubert So the Mexicans are at it!

Henri That's right!

Hubert Troublesome?

Henri I hope not. I don't know what their approach is or their conclusion, Raoul's going to call me back. There's a good chance we may complement each other.

Hubert Yes, yes, yes. I'm sure you will.

Henri Let's put our trust in the diversity of the human brain.

Hubert Well done.

Henri I shall have to incorporate their results in my paper. Might even be an advantage.

Hubert Of course! I must say, Henri, you're on very good form.

Henri Exhausted, but, yes, on good form.

Hubert Nice part of town.

Henri Very.

Sonia appears.

Sonia He wants you to come.

Henri I'd rather he went to sleep.

Sonia He's showing Inès his airport and he says you haven't seen it.

Henri Would you excuse me for two minutes, Hubert?

He goes out.
Hubert and Sonia are on their own.
Immediately, Hubert throws himself at Sonia and tries to take her in his arms.

Hubert Half-undressed, no make-up, in your flat, surrounded by your things, you couldn't have done better if you'd set out to knock me sideways . . .

Sonia (*laughing and trying – feebly – to get away from him*) You're bonkers . . .

Hubert (*pursuing her*) You're adorable, Sonia, you're heart-breaking, you're disarming . . . I didn't run here, I flew here, I blasted a day out of the calendar, I dismantled time to get back by your side . . .

Sonia You've seen me twice in your life . . . you're drunk . . .

Hubert So? Once would have been enough . . .

He tries to kiss her, misses. She laughs, pulls away. He catches hold of her hand, playful.

. . . Do you know the Baltic? . . . Last month I went for a walk north of Turku, through cold and desolate countryside, and all I could think of was a woman glimpsed when I was visiting those unfortunate Blochs . . .

She manages to escape, but he recaptures her.

. . . I was walking beside a dark sea, beside low houses with no windows, and I couldn't stop thinking of her . . . what a lucky man Henri is, Henri is magnificent, some Mexicans have covered his subject, he's pretending he couldn't care less, but if they refuse to publish his paper, there's nothing I can do for him . . . I worship your eyes . . .

Sonia Mexicans?

Hubert Mexicans.

Sonia They're the other side of that door . . .

Hubert The Mexicans?

Sonia laughs and lets herself be caught.

Sonia . . . My son, Henri, Inès . . .

Hubert The whole world is on the other side of that door . . . the world is always on the other side of the door! . . .

He kisses her. She lets him do it.
The voices of Inès and Henri can be heard.
They pull apart.

Inès He's a real architect, that child!

Henri He wants a biscuit.

Hubert (*grabbing the packet of chocolate fingers*) Here, take it, they'll be the death of me, these chocolate fingers!

Inès Really, Hubert, they're not going to give him a packet of biscuits in bed!

Henri Not even one!

Sonia Give it to him, what harm can it do, it's not going to kill him.

Henri Give him the whole packet?

Hubert I've eaten three-quarters of them.

Inès (*to Henri, who's about to leave the room with the packet*) You shouldn't, Henri.

Henri What shall I do?!

Sonia Give him a biscuit.

Henri Just one?

Hubert There can't be more than two or three left in the packet.

Henri What shall I do, Sonia, before I go crazy?

Sonia Give him what's left and tell him it'll never happen again.

Henri goes out.

Inès He explained everything to me. In fact, he's built an air station!

Hubert An airport.

Inès No, no, an air station.

Hubert The word is airport.

Inès I know perfectly well what an airport is, Hubert, but the child has built an air station, a station inside an airport, a station with trains, with rails crossing the runways, it's not an airport, it's an air terminal with aeroplanes, combined with a railway station and he calls it an air station!

Henri (*coming back*) There were two chocolate fingers left!

Inès What is that thing Arnaud has made? An air station!

Henri That's right, an air station.

Hubert All right. No need to get annoyed.

Henri Who's getting annoyed? You must be dying of thirst out here. Something stronger, Hubert?

Hubert No, thanks, I'll stick with the Sancerre.

Henri (*serving him*) Sonia? . . . Inès? . . .

He fills everyone's glass.
Silence.

Hubert What's become of the Blochs? Have you seen them?

Sonia They've been flooded out.

Hubert Flooded out?

Sonia The kid upstairs, before he went on holiday, watered his plants and left the tap on.

Henri Francine had just redecorated.

Sonia And he'd just come out of a depression.

Hubert Poor man's a depressive.

Henri Yes.

Pause.

Hubert The last time I saw him, I said, listen, Serge, depression is a spiral, no one can help you, no one can do a thing for you, the only cure is willpower, willpower, willpower. After that, he was three times worse. Not at all the right thing to say to him. He was prostrate when I left, I've never seen anyone look so terrified.

Inès If I was depressed and somebody said to me willpower, willpower, I'd jump straight out of a window.

Sonia Me too.

Hubert What can you say? You're on a losing wicket whatever you do. You could say you're a length ahead, old man, you've pre-empted the inevitable decay, well done, be grateful to your destiny for giving you the edge in this kingdom of the damned. You could say that.

Silence.

Henri We ought to ask the Blochs for dinner.

Sonia Any other brilliant ideas?

The telephone rings.
Henri answers it.

Henri Hello, yes . . . (*to the others*) It's Raoul Arestegui . . .
(*to Raoul*) Yes . . . yes . . . Right. Really? . . . Really! . . .
No, no, I dealt with three of the external galaxies! . . .
You said it! . . . One to ten . . . Three to four? . . . Good,
wonderful . . . Thanks, Raoul, thank you, I can't talk
now, I'm with some friends, see you Monday . . . Ciao.
(*He hangs up.*) 'On the Flatness of the Milky Way's Dark
Halo'! The Milky Way! They've dealt with the Milky
Way! . . . Cosmological simulations give a ratio of one to
two! My ratio is one to ten! And the Mexicans' results
are three to four!

Hubert Marvellous.

Henri (*quietly crazed with joy*) Not so marvellous but
I do feel better! Come on everyone, drink up! Here's to
the Mexicans! You must be starving to death, aren't
you? Sonia, where are those Wotsits, didn't we have
some Wotsits, darling?

Sonia There.

Henri Ah, I hadn't spotted them! Prawn cocktail
Wotsits, barbecue Wotsits! Barbecue, fabulous, Inès?

Inès No, thank you.

Henri Come on, Hubert, tuck in!

Hubert takes a handful of Wotsits and raises his glass.

Hubert To the publication of your paper, Henri!

Henri (*clinking his glass, happy*) He's taking the piss,
but I don't mind!

Inès I don't know what you're talking about, but here's to you anyway!

Sonia Here's to you and here's a kiss, my darling.

Henri Yes, give us a kiss, my darling! And we'll raise our glasses to the hero of the hour, that colossus who's published nothing for three years and who's painting the town red because he's able to submit his little paper!

Sonia Don't be so coy!

Henri Not coy. Flippant, Sonia. I don't want our friends to think that in spite of my relief, I've lost all sense of proportion. (*He drinks.*) Especially in front of a pundit.

Hubert He's taking the piss, but what do I care?

Sonia You're not a pundit? I'd be very disappointed.

Henri Be careful, I've steeped her in the myth of Finidori.

Hubert I see.

Henri The Milky Way! Idiot, why didn't he tell me right away? Here I was, worrying about spiral galaxies and elliptical galaxies! Some music? Let's put on some music!

Inès Oh, yes, some music!

Sonia We're not putting on any music, Henri!

Henri Why not?

Hubert He's right, why not?

Henri No, of course, this is silly, we shouldn't put on any music.

Inès Why shouldn't we put on some music?

Hubert He doesn't want to any more, Inès.

Sonia We can spend an enjoyable evening without music, can't we?

Inès You seem depressed, all of a sudden, Henri.

Henri I'm not depressed.

Inès Your son has created a wonderful thing, he'll destroy it tomorrow, you don't keep things in his world, you keep nothing, not even yourself . . . (*She drinks.*) . . . Pour me another drink, please, Henri, I feel low all of a sudden, so low I'm afraid I might ruin your evening . . . He made snow on the runways with paper handkerchiefs . . . above the building bricks the storms and hurricanes rage . . . above our heads . . . there's what? . . . You people who dwell among the stars, give me a dream to cling to.

Henri I don't dwell among the stars, Inès . . . Far lower down, if you want to know the truth.

Inès Really?

Henri As you can see. Sliding from an absurd euphoria to an equally absurd melancholy. It's all built on nothing.

Slight pause.

Hubert In any case, Henri, getting back to your paper, providing you publish before the end of the year, I'll make a point of mentioning you to the Committee.

Henri No obligation whatsoever, Hubert.

Sonia Henri, are you sure you haven't had a bit too much to drink?

Hubert I shall mention you, because you're very pure, you're talented but not in the least aggressive. You don't have the strategic capabilities of a number of your colleagues. A career is a plan of campaign.

Henri Put that way, it makes me want to puke.

Hubert In that case, I shall mention you in order to get into Sonia's good books, since I get the impression she doesn't like me.

Inès You think you're witty but you're utterly predictable.

Sonia The elegant way to go about it would have been to support my husband without letting him know. A discreet leg-up.

Hubert So you don't like me.

Henri Who wants the last barbecue-flavoured Wotsit?

Hubert You eat it, Henri.

Pause.

Henri The barbecue-flavoured ones are my favourites.

Hubert For me, the discovery of the evening was . . . what are they called? . . . the chocolate fingers. Make a note of them, Inès.

Henri You'll be able to brag about going to the shittiest dinner party of your life.

Hubert This sudden bout of gloom, Henri, give me a hint. Is it something we said?

Sonia Henri wants things to happen and he wants them not to happen. He wants to succeed and at the same time not to succeed, to be somebody and to be nobody. To be you, Hubert, and to be a failure, he wants to be helped and he wants to be rejected. That's Henri for you, Hubert, a man who slides from euphoria to melancholy and from melancholy back to euphoria, who suddenly gets excited, leaps out of bed and gets excited and thinks life is full of promise and sees himself getting the Russell Prize or the Nobel, assumes a feverishly conspiratorial air, then, suddenly, for no reason, is overwhelmed and paralysed, so that haste and impatience are replaced by doubt and insecurity and desire is replaced by doubt and boundless insecurity, some people can cope with life and some people can't . . .

Inès I've laddered my stocking.

Henri She used to be a lawyer before she went to work for the finance company. If you ask me, any criminal you can think of, she would have him got off.

Hubert Why don't you put your glass down, Inès?

Inès I've gone downhill this last two hours. Did you know Hubert's just been elected to the Academy of Science?

Silence.

Sonia You've just been elected to the Academy of Science?

Hubert You don't have to shout it from the rooftops.

Inès This isn't the rooftops, don't be rude, these are our friends.

Hubert Our friends couldn't care less.

Sonia Your friends could care less, Hubert, your friends – if the word is not an exaggeration – your friends are most impressed. They bow their heads. They would like to share your delight but . . .

Henri They do share your delight, well done, Hubert, what's she talking about?!

Sonia They do share your delight, yes.

Henri We share your delight. The Academy, what an achievement, Hubert! And here are we celebrating the Academy with crisps and Wotsits! We do share your delight, and even if this evening I'm suddenly prone, you know, to some slight feeling of isolation, I'm delighted, Hubert, sincerely I am, at your apotheosis.

Hubert Apotheosis. Right. (*He gets up.*) Inès. It's late, we must be on our way.

Inès gets up.

Hubert I shall speak to the Committee about you, Henri. Discreetly. Send me your paper even before you submit it.

Inès Thanks for a lovely evening. It's time I went, only needs one glass to make me feel squiffy.

Hubert See you Sonia . . .

Sonia See you . . .

> *They leave.*
> *Henri and Sonia are on their own.*
> *Silence.*

Henri Is he asleep?

Sonia Think so.

> *The Fox and the Hound music is heard, coming from the child's room.*